# Consent
## Deal with it
### before boundaries get crossed

**Keisha Evans** and **N.B. Gonsalvez**
Illustrated by Jenny Chan, The Public Studio

James Lorimer & Company Ltd., Publishers
Toronto

In the basketball game, you score the winning basket for your team! Your teammates run over to you, cheering and giving you high-fives. One of your teammates slaps you on your butt. He slaps everyone on the team on the butt. It shouldn't be a big deal for you, right? You don't say anything to your teammate, but you feel really uncomfortable. You understand that his slap is just to say you had a good game. But it bothers you. You didn't tell him he could do that.

# Do people have the right to make you feel uncomfortable or awkward by the actions they display toward you?

## What does it mean to give and have consent? Does consent always have to be given for everything?

If you have ever felt embarrassed or awkward because of someone's actions toward you and you did not know what to do, then this book can help you understand the importance of setting boundaries, setting limits, having mutual respect, and giving and having consent.

Contents

# What is Consent?

Everyone has the right to choose what they want to do or what they want to happen to them and their body.

**We all know that we need permission to:**

- be touched
- touch others
- share secrets
- kiss
- hug
- be intimate with someone
- touch someone in private places
- have sex

**But what about:**

- holding hands?
- saying you are in a relationship?
- borrowing something?
- handling someone's possessions?
- touching in non-private places?
- sharing something?
- posting a picture of someone online?
- watching private content?
- telling someone's story?
- speaking on someone's behalf?

Getting consent is something that everyone needs to practise doing. And everyone has a right to say no. You have the right to make your own decisions when it comes to you. When people don't get consent for their actions, that's where conflict can begin.

# Consent 101

Consent can be . . .

By going to see Dr. Kent, Jack is giving consent for her to do what she needs to treat him.

It sounds like you have a bad cold. If it doesn't get better in a few days, come back and see me.

Are they allowed to go through our things without asking?

By going through customs, Bobby and his family imply their consent to having whatever they are taking across the border inspected.

# Consent 101

Consent needs to be given so that everyone knows what the boundaries are. There are times when consent is needed and not needed. Read the following scenarios and decide if consent is needed or not.

## 1 Car Trouble

Farique and his dad are out when their car breaks down. When they get to the garage, the mechanic opens the hood and starts checking the engine of the car.

**Consent is not needed.** When you take your car to a mechanic, it is assumed you are consenting to having it checked out and repaired.

## 2 Styling

Selena's stylist tells her there is a great style that would be perfect for Selena. She wants to cut Selena's hair short and colour it red.

**Consent is needed.** The hairdresser can offer their opinion, but it's up to Selena to make the final decision of what she wants for herself.

## 3 The Cavity

Elijah goes to the dentist with his mom. The dentist tells Elijah's mom that Elijah has three cavities that need to be filled.

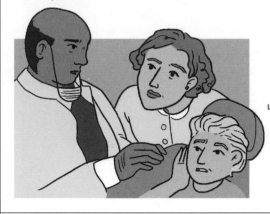

**Consent is not needed.** Elijah's is a minor and his mom needs to be informed that Elijah has cavities. consent is not needed for the dentist to share this information.

## 4 The Secret Crush

Tony has a crush on Riley. He tells Stuart not to tell anyone, but Stuart is dying to tell Mike.

**Consent is needed.** Tony did not give Stuart consent to share his secret.

## 5 Teacher, Teacher

No one knows that Shanisse is failing her Math class. She doesn't want anyone to know that she needs extra help. However, Shanisse's teacher tells her parents about her grades.

**Consent is not needed.** For students under the age of 18, a teacher does not need consent to speak to their parents.

## 6  The Borrower

Michael sees that D'neice has a video game in her backpack that Michael is dying to play, so Michael takes it.

**Consent is needed.** Michael needs permission to borrow the video game.

## 7  Body Language

Rachel and Ahmed are making out. Rachel starts becoming uncomfortable and tells Ahmed to stop. Ahmed says he can tell that Rachel likes it and wants to go on.

**Consent is needed.** Even if making out with Ahmed feels good to Rachel, she has the right to stop what is happening as soon as anything doesn't feel right to her.

## 8  Driving Mom Crazy

River's mom is mad at her because she took the car. River knows that her mom always lets her take the car when she asks for it, so this time she just took it.

**Consent is needed.** River needs permission every time to borrow the car. Permission should not be assumed.

## 9  The Conversation

Aaliyah overhears her mother talking to her aunt in Trinidad. Aaliyah's mom is sharing a private conversation Aaliyah had with her.

**Consent is needed.** Aaliyah's mom needs Aaliyah's consent because it was not her story to share.

## 10  The Camper

Jason's class is going on a camping trip, but he forgot his permission form at home.

**Consent is needed.** Parents need to provide written or verbal consent for Jason to go on a trip with the school.

# Dear Conflict Counsellor

**Q.** My mother brought her boyfriend over to our house. In his culture everyone kisses each other on the cheek to greet one another. Mom explained that it is seen as a gesture of friendship and comfort. Every time he comes over, he hugs me and kisses me on the cheek. The problem is that I am really uncomfortable with him doing that. What should I do?

— *Feeling the Culture Clash*

**A.** I know you want your mom to be happy. It is not always easy to tell someone how you are feeling, especially if you think it will offend them. But it is important that you do what is comfortable for you, even though you may think that you might be hurting your mom's boyfriend's feelings or your mom's.

**Q:** I agreed to meet up with this guy I met online. He seemed really nice when I spoke to him on the phone. But on our date, this guy kept grabbing my butt and it made me feel really uncomfortable and awkward. I told him to stop. He told me if I didn't want him to grab my butt, then I shouldn't have worn tight jeans. Is that true? Did I ask for it?

— *Swiping Right*

**A:** It is your right to wear what you want. The clothes you wear do not define who you are and definitely do not give consent for you to be treated in a certain way. And agreeing to meet does not give this guy the right to touch you without getting your permission. What happened to you is not your fault.

**Q:** My soccer coach is only a few years older than me. He always tells me how pretty I am. After every practice, he always takes me for a treat. The last time he offered to drive me home. Before we got to my place, he pulled over and kissed me on the lips. I was shocked and felt uncomfortable. I don't want to get him in trouble because he is my coach. Did I do something wrong? Should I tell someone?

— *Unwanted Pass*

**A:** It is not okay when someone you trust or who is in a position of authority uses their power to get you to do something you are not comfortable doing. You did not do anything wrong. You should tell a trusted adult and seek help.

**Q:** My best friend and I got into an argument. She decided to post our private conversation online to get everyone on her side. Now everyone thinks I am the bad friend. What should I do? Should I post my side of what happened?

— *The Losing Side*

**A:** Posting private conversations online without permission is never okay. It can get you in a lot of trouble. Consent must be given because conversations are considered private. Try talking to your friend. Ask her to take the conversation down and try to resolve the situation.

# Myths

## If you say yes, it means you can't change your mind.

Even if you start off by saying yes, you can change your mind at any time and take back your consent.

## It's not **stealing** if I give it back.

If you "borrow" something without the owner's consent, then it's theft.

## Rape is **always** an attack by a **stranger** in a **dark alley**.

Any sexual contact — with anyone, anywhere — without consent is sexual assault.

## DID YOU KNOW?

- The word *consent* comes from the Latin word *consentire*, meaning agreeing to give permission.

# If you ask **permission** to kiss, people will think you are **weird**.

It may feel awkward and uncomfortable at first, but consent is still required to kiss. People will see that they'd rather kiss someone who respects their rights!

## People who wear revealing clothes want to be **noticed** and **touched**.

People can choose to wear whatever they want without having to worry about others making assumptions.

---

- You need consent to record and share personal phone calls.

- According to the law, young people under the age of 18 cannot consent to a nude image of themselves being taken or shared with another person.

# The **Choice Maker**

It's not like you have a phobia of people touching you.

You are okay with the occasional hug. But what's wrong with just a wave to say hello? Why does everyone have to be so touchy and feely? You wish people would ask you if it's okay to hug you or to kiss you on the cheek. You wish there was a way to tell people not to do things that make you uncomfortable. But you want them to keep liking you. You don't want them to think you are rude or stand-offish.

# DEAR DR. SHRINK-WRAPPED...

**Q.** My girlfriend and I do a lot of sexting. One time I sent her a video and she decided to show it to her friends without my permission. She didn't think it was a big deal, but I am upset. I don't want all those girls seeing what is private between my girlfriend and me. It is a big deal to me. What should I do? What should I say to her?

— *Exposed*

**A.** It's too bad that your girlfriend violated your privacy. Even though you consented to texting by giving her the video, you did not consent for her to distribute it. In fact, Exposed, what your girlfriend did is a crime. You both need to speak to a trusted adult and together decide what to do.

# dos and don'ts

✓ Do voice your choice and make it clear

✓ Do know you have a right to say yes or no

✓ Do report to someone if you feel that you have been violated

✓ Do trust your gut feeling

✓ Do know that you can change your mind at any time

✓ Do know you have support

✓ Do know about your consent rights

✗ Don't let others make decisions for you

✗ Don't be afraid to say no

✗ Don't feel bad for your decisions

✗ Don't second-guess yourself

✗ Don't feel pressured into a decision you are not comfortable with

✗ Don't feel that you have to be pressured into doing something

✗ Don't be afraid to say what you want and don't want

✗ Don't hesitate to ask for help

✗ Don't be afraid to set boundaries

# QUIZ

## It's all about your right to choose.

Do you find that your personal space is always violated? Are you tired of having your personal belongings or right to choose taken away? Consent is everything, and you have your own way of dealing with it. You can **Speak Up** and let the other person know what your choice is. You can **Get Up** and remove yourself from the situation. Or you might just **Give Up** your choice and allow it to be made for you. Take this quiz, then check out your answers to see what your consent style is.

**Speak Up**

**Get Up**

**Give Up**

## 1 Get the Massage

You are in the library doing homework. A friend approaches you from behind and starts to massage your shoulders. Do you a) tell him to stop? b) collect your books and leave the library? or c) sit there and let him continue even though it makes you uncomfortable?

a) Speak Up    b) Get Up    c) Give Up

## 2 Brother Bother

Your brother knows that you hate when he uses your belongings without your permission. One night when you are half-asleep, he asks to use your phone and takes it. When you wake up, you realize that your phone is missing. Do you a) grab your phone from him? b) get upset and tell him that you did not give true consent because you were asleep? or c) accept that you gave him permission and let him use your phone?

a) Get Up    b) Speak Up    c) Give Up

## 3 Ready or Not

You invite your boyfriend to your place while your parents are out. You and he have kissed before, but now you don't feel ready to do anything more than holding hands and hugging. When you tell him that, he gets mad and starts to kiss and touch you. What do you do? a) Kick him out. b) Let him keep on doing what he is doing; after all, you gave consent before. c) Stop him and have a conversation about how, even though you let him kiss you before, you are saying no now.

a) Get Up    b) Give Up    c) Speak Up

## 4 Cineplex

Your friends want to go to the movies and have chosen what they want to see. You have already seen the movie, but one friend says that she knows you well enough and has agreed to the choice without you. What do you do? a) Just go. It's not worth the trouble to go against them. b) Tell them you are not going and walk away. c) Tell your friends that you saw that movie already and ask them to choose something else to watch.

a) Give Up    b) Get Up    c) Speak Up

## 5 Kiss, Kiss

You and your friend Monique go to get something to eat at your favourite restaurant. When saying goodbye you go to hug her, and she quickly kisses you on the lips. Do you a) continue to kiss, even though you did not like it? b) tell her that you are not okay with it and she should have asked first? or c) back away and leave upset?

a) Give Up    b) Speak Up    c) Get Up

## 6 Secret Sharer

You tell your friend Cheyenne a secret that no one else knows and you ask her not to tell anyone. You later find out that Cheyenne told another friend. Do you a) ask Cheyenne why she shared your secret? b) say nothing to Cheyenne, but know you will never share another secret with her again? or c) confront Cheyenne angrily and dissolve the friendship?

a) Speak Up    b) Give Up    c) Get Up

## 7 Rugby Scrum

Hannah is a student-teacher and also coaches the boy's rugby team. It has been noticed that Hannah has offered to give private coaching lessons to some of the players she especially likes. One evening after school you ask for help with your catches. Hannah gets closer to you than she needs to and keeps touching you in ways you don't like. Do you a) tell her to stop because what she is doing is making you uncomfortable? b) push her away and leave? or c) let her continue because you are scared you will get kicked off the team?

a) Speak Up    b) Get Up    c) Give Up

## 8 Friends with Benefits

You are at the park with your friend Courtney. He leans over and starts to kiss you. You are really enjoying it. Courtney then starts to touch you. At first you like how that feels, but it becomes too much for you. You feel like you are losing control. So, you ask Courtney to stop. Courtney doesn't stop. Do you a) pull away? b) tell him again to stop? c) just go with it?

a) Get Up    b) Speak Up    c) Give Up

## 9 Bedroom Basics

Your friend Luciana comes over to help you with homework, but your brother is watching TV in the family room and your dad is making dinner in the kitchen. So, you take Luciana up to your bedroom to work. As soon as you get there, she closes the door and says that she knew you wanted to be alone with her. She says you owe her a kiss for her help with your homework. What do you do? a) Tell her that you invited her to your room to work, not to make out. b) Let her kiss you so that you can get her help with your homework. c) Pick up your books and look for somewhere else to work.

a) Speak Up    b) Give Up    c) Get Up

## 10 Tackling Dummy

When you play tackle football with Selim, you do not like the inappropriate touching from Selim when he tackles you. Do you a) continue playing the game, even though you do not like the way Selim touches you? b) quit the game and walk away? or c) tell Selim you are going to play only if he plays by the rules?

a) Give Up    b) Get Up    c) Speak Up

# Time to take back the taking.

There are some basic things you can do to ensure you are asked for your consent every time.

**Make your choice**
People need to know what you are comfortable with. If you do not choose what you want for yourself, it allows others to come into your personal space and violate your right to choose what happens to you.

**Use your words**
Some people do not like to hear the word no. So, they might try to persuade you to say yes. Make sure you voice your choice and be clear. Try telling people respectfully what you do not like and what makes you feel uncomfortable. If you use clear words, such as "no," "stop," "don't," they may just listen and back off.

**Stand your ground**
Be firm with your decision. If the behaviour continues, tell whoever is taking advantage of you that the friendship or relationship will end if they cannot respect your choices.

**Enough is enough**
If people continue to not respect your choices, you have to stop them from treating you without respect. Depending on the circumstances, you might have to walk away, tell a trusted adult, or even call the police.

## DID YOU KNOW?

- Sex between two people consenting to have sex is called "consensual sex."
- According to Statistics Canada, six per cent of males 15 or older reported that they had experienced sexual victimization.

# When Sex is Involved

Consent is very important, especially when sex is involved. It is of the utmost importance to always make sure to receive consent when engaging in sexual activities. If consent is not given during any sexual activity and the action of engaging in sexual activity is not stopped, it is a crime. Some people think that consent is not always needed. Consent is always needed. Even when consent has been given, the person giving the consent (the choice maker) always has a right to change their mind. Once they change their mind, the action must be stopped immediately.

## Age of Consent

The legal age of consent in Canada is 16 years old. Anyone under the age of 16 cannot legally give consent. That means that having sex with someone younger than 16 is against the law, even if the person agrees to it. Like most things in life, there are exceptions to this rule.

Persons under 16 years old can have consensual sex with someone close to their age:

• For people 12–13 years old, there can be a two-year age difference
• For people 14–15 years old, there can be a five-year age difference

Persons under the age of 18 cannot consent to sexual activity if
• the other consenting party is in a position of trust or authority, or there is a dependency on that person
• exploitation is present. Examples of exploitation are prostitution, pornography, and/or sex work.

# When consent is not given

Sexual assault is any unwanted act of a sexual nature that is imposed on another person without their consent. This is not limited to being violated by a stranger; it can be someone you know, even someone you have a relationship with. You always have the right to refuse consent to sex with anyone, at any time, for any reason.
If you have ever been sexually assaulted:

• remember, you have the right to report it to the police, regardless of how long ago the sexual assault was.
• you have a right to seek out medical attention at any time, even if you decide not to report it to the police.
• know your rights and if you are unsure if your consent has been violated, seek help from an adult who you trust. Consent starts with you.

• Nigeria, an African nation, has the lowest age of consent in the world at 11 years old.

• Bahrain, a country in Asia, has the highest legal age of consent at 21 years old.

# The **Consent Taker**

# Do you like to **hug people, and** sometimes **give them a kiss?**

Does it bug you that people are so sensitive about their personal space? **Why do you need to ask** someone permission to do something nice to them or even **touch** their hair?

What's the big deal if you share someone else's secret with a close friend — it's not like you're telling everyone. Why is getting consent such a big deal?

# DEAR DR. SHRINK-WRAPPED...

**Q:** I have this friend who is really uptight. She thinks everyone has to ask her for permission to touch her hair or hug her. She says she doesn't like people in her personal space and they have to ask her for her consent to even talk to her. I swear she thinks she is better than everyone else. Really, what is the big deal? Why do I need permission to hug or even talk to someone? It's harmless, right?

— *Just Being Friendly*

**A:** Everyone has the right to their own personal space. Some may like you close, Friendly, while others may prefer you farther away. Your friend has as much right to who she invites into her personal space as you have to ask to be included in that. Try asking her for permission, it might not be so bad.

**Q:** Last week I was going out with my friends and I couldn't find anything to wear. My sister has the best clothes and there was this dress of hers I was dying to wear. She wasn't home for me to ask, so I just took it. I figured I would put it back when I got home and she would never know I borrowed it. While I was out, I spilled grape juice all over it. My sister is going to be so mad. The dress was brand new and she has never worn it before. I tried washing it but the grape juice left a stain and it won't come out. What should I do?

— *Scared Sister*

**A:** Honesty is the best policy. You know that you should not have taken your sister's dress without her permission. Any time you take something without permission, it's actually theft, even if it is from your sister. Own up and say you're a Sorry Sister. Maybe if you suggest that you will replace her dress with a new one, you won't have to be a Scared one.

# QUIZ

## Are you a taker?

Do you think that everyone should just calm down about how they are treated? Are you taking away people's right — or even your own — to choose for themselves? Take this quiz to see what you can find out about yourself. Of the following statements, how many are true, and how many are false?

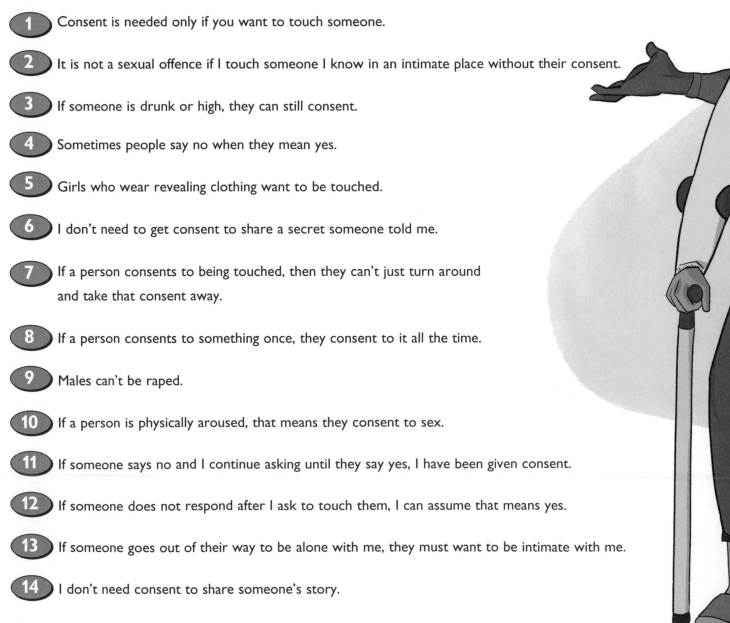

1. Consent is needed only if you want to touch someone.

2. It is not a sexual offence if I touch someone I know in an intimate place without their consent.

3. If someone is drunk or high, they can still consent.

4. Sometimes people say no when they mean yes.

5. Girls who wear revealing clothing want to be touched.

6. I don't need to get consent to share a secret someone told me.

7. If a person consents to being touched, then they can't just turn around and take that consent away.

8. If a person consents to something once, they consent to it all the time.

9. Males can't be raped.

10. If a person is physically aroused, that means they consent to sex.

11. If someone says no and I continue asking until they say yes, I have been given consent.

12. If someone does not respond after I ask to touch them, I can assume that means yes.

13. If someone goes out of their way to be alone with me, they must want to be intimate with me.

14. I don't need consent to share someone's story.

**15** I don't need consent to kiss the person I am dating.

 **16** I don't need consent to borrow something from my best friend.

**17** I don't need consent to borrow something I've borrowed before.

**18** I don't need consent to post a picture of my friend on social media.

 **19** I can speak for my friend without checking to see how they feel about something.

 **20** I can give consent for someone else.

**21** Giving consent can be done through actions.

 **22** I cannot change my mind once I have given my consent.

**23** No one really objects to a hug.

 **24** If I borrow something, it doesn't mean I am stealing.

**25** If someone flirts with me, it means that they are open for a kiss.

If you answered **TRUE** to a lot of these statements, go back and read why consent is so important. Try to imagine what it would feel like if you were not given the right to decide what you want for yourself. Without consent, how could you ever get the chance to voice your choice?

# The Consent Taker

# Everyone has boundaries — yes, even you.

Boundaries are limits you put in place between you and another person. These limits can be mental, emotional, and physical. It is important for you to listen to what a person's boundaries are and respect them. It is equally important to ask if you are unsure. Consent must always be given. We cannot assume what the other person wants or likes, so communication is the key.

**Imagine** people doing things to you that you do not like. Not everyone shares the same comfort level as you do, so it is important to have mutual respect and look at things from their point of view.

**Ask** for consent. It's a great way to keep any relationship healthy. Being able to communicate honestly and openly is a great way to establish trust. It's not just about asking, it's about making sure everyone is happy and comfortable. Do you want to . . . ? Can I . . . ? Can we . . . ? Are you comfortable with . . . ? These are all great ways to start to ask for consent.

**Accept the answer, whatever it is.** Be okay with hearing the word "no." If someone says no, believe them the first time, and don't keep trying to hear what you want. Do not assume that silence means yes. It's better to assume that silence means no.

**Talk** about what everyone is comfortable with. Agree to kiss, touch, hug, or share. True consent should never be forced and always needs to be freely given and clear. Remember that consent is an ongoing conversation. Getting consent is required every time. It is not only respectful, it is the law.

## DID YOU KNOW?

- In Canada, fewer than one in ten sexual assault survivors report the crime to the police. Only about 2 per cent of sexual assault reports are false.

24

✓ Do make sure to get consent, even just to get a hug

✓ Do know it's okay to hear the word "no"

✓ Do communicate about what you and the other person are comfortable with

✓ Do respect personal boundaries

✓ Do know a person who is under the influence cannot give consent

✓ Do understand that if someone is quiet or seems unsure, that is not consent

✓ Do know that consent is an ongoing conversation

✓ Do respect the choices made by others

✓ Do be patient

✓ Do know that "no" is not about you; it's about what someone is comfortable with

✗ Don't keep trying to get a "yes"; this is called coercion

✗ Don't make assumptions about what someone wants

✗ Don't take what doesn't belong to you

✗ Don't take things personally

✗ Don't make someone feel guilty or bad for their choices

✗ Don't assume that everyone enjoys being touched

✗ Don't share secrets told to you by others

✗ Don't be afraid to ask for clarification if you are unsure of what is being said

✗ Don't force your choices on others

✗ Don't end healthy relationships because someone says no

**Act** only after getting permission to. Actions have consequences. If you do not get consent and you proceed, you could end up being charged with a criminal offence. So, think before you act!

- Consent is not just about hearing the word no, but about getting an enthusiastic yes.

- Indigenous people were forbidden by law to practise their traditions and speak their languages, so it's important not to share their stories without their consent.

# You don't like to get involved in anyone else's business.

But has it bothered you to see people made uncomfortable by an unwanted action toward them?

Have you seen someone get upset because someone shared their secret or took something of theirs without permission?

**You realize that people should speak up when these sorts of incidents happen to them, but did you say or do anything? Well, why not?**

# Consent to be a hero.

It's not always easy to make the right choice, especially when you are placed in a situation where you have to decide whether or not to speak up for someone else. But when you speak up to help other people, you are being a voice for those who are too scared or intimidated to speak for themselves. You can empower others and help them to feel safe. You are also helping to change people's views on consent and showing everyone how important consent really is!

# Know your limits.

Sometimes speaking up is just too challenging and that is okay. Live to fight another day! Consent is about setting boundaries and limits. For your safety and the safety of others, it is important to know your own limits and boundaries and assess the situation. Sometimes getting help or walking away is the best thing you can do for everyone. Whatever you decide, whether it be speaking up, getting help, or walking away, let people know why you made your choice, so they, too, can consent to be a hero!

## dos and don'ts

- ✓ Do encourage people to seek help
- ✓ Do support others if they are being treated in a way they don't like
- ✓ Do give people space to decide for themselves
- ✓ Do listen and be respectful
- ✓ Do establish a buddy system when going out
- ✓ Do know that you have a choice to speak up if you feel safe doing so
- ✓ Do understand that everyone has different limits and boundaries; what may be comfortable for you may be uncomfortable for your friend
- ✓ Do know your voice is powerful and can help

- ✗ Don't make decisions for others
- ✗ Don't minimize what others are going through or how they are feeling
- ✗ Don't blame someone if something has happened to them
- ✗ Don't share other people's secrets
- ✗ Don't forget to take care of yourself
- ✗ Don't pressure people to do what they are uncomfortable with
- ✗ Don't be afraid to stand up for what is right
- ✗ Don't think that you can solve someone else's issue by yourself
- ✗ Don't blame yourself for others' choices

27

# The Witness

# QUIZ

Sometimes it can be hard to know when to get involved. Sometimes there is no perfect way to react. But you do have choices! Each of these situations has several possible options and no answer is right or wrong. You might even come up with a different solution that works for you.

## 1 Lunchtime Hero

You and your friend Yasmina are having lunch in the school cafeteria when she starts getting harassed by another group of kids. They are making rude sexual comments and your friend is getting upset.

- Keep eating and tell Yasmina to ignore them.
- Ask the group to stop making inappropriate comments to your friend.
- Get your friend and move away from the situation.
- Find a trusted teacher or member of the school staff and tell them what is happening.

## 2 Party Central

You and Mae are best friends. At a party, you see Mae drinking and acting silly, and you know that she has had too much to drink. You see that Mohammed, a boy Mae has a crush on, is also pretty drunk, and he approaches her. Mohammed holds Mae by her hand and starts leading her upstairs.

- Let Mae go with Mohammed; she likes him.
- Plan to go and check on Mae in a while.
- Stop them and tell them that no one is allowed upstairs.
- Step in and tell both of them they shouldn't do things when they are drunk.
- Grab Mae and convince her to leave the party with you.
- Find an adult and tell them things are out of control.

## 3  The Survivor

Your friend Becky tells you that she has been raped by her uncle.

- Ask your friend how you can help and support her.
- Listen to Becky and validate her feelings.
- Ask Becky if she wants you to keep her secret or to share it with someone you trust.
- Encourage her to seek professional help and offer to help find other resources for her.
- Tell a trusted adult.

## 4  Brotherly Love

Ali tells you that a girl put her hands down his pants and he didn't like it. He asked her to stop and she didn't. He told his brothers, and they just laughed at him and told him that what happened was every guy's dream.

- Assure your friend that not every guy wants to be violated.
- Tell him that telling her to stop was the right thing to do.
- If the situation affected him, encourage him to seek help.
- Ask a teacher or school counsellor if a session can be arranged to learn about consent.
- Tell a trusted adult.

## 5  The Conversation

You're at your volunteer job and you overhear other volunteers, who go to the same school as you, talking about a girl who got sexually assaulted. They said she asked for it because she always wears short skirts and tight tops.

- Try to ignore them.
- Interrupt the conversation and tell them that no one asks to be sexually assaulted.
- Advise your manager of what was said and ask them to have a talk with the other volunteers about what is appropriate talk.
- Talk to your school counsellor about the incident.

Continues . . .

## 6 *The Sound of Silence*

Morgan is a special-needs girl in your class. She is non-verbal, but you notice that every time the other girls play with her hair, she seems to get agitated.

- Keep it to yourself; you don't want to make Morgan even more embarrassed by calling attention to it.
- Explain to the girls that Morgan may not like that and that they need to get consent to touch her.
- Ask the teacher to talk about consent to the class so that they know how important consent is for everyone.
- Speak to Morgan's caregivers about ways to help her communicate what she wants.

## 7 *Joy Rider*

Your older sister Joy always takes your mom's car without her permission. You see your sister take the keys and drive away one night when your mom is sleeping.

- Do nothing; the car will be back by the time your mom wakes up, and you don't want your sister mad at you.
- Wait up for Joy and tell her that it is wrong for her to take the car without getting your mom's consent.
- Mention to Joy that if she gets caught with the car without your mom's permission, she can be charged with stealing the car.
- Tell Joy that if it happens again, you will tell your mom.

## DID YOU KNOW?

- If you share a picture or video of someone without permission from the person who took it, is a breach of copyright.

## 8 Tickle, Tickle

Jenna shares with you that her friend Jess thinks it's fun to greet Jenna by tickling her, but Jenna says that she is really uncomfortable with it. She doesn't want to hurt her friend's feelings, even though it triggers her.

- Sympathize, but do nothing; this is a secret Jenna has shared with you.
- Have a conversation with Jess about Jenna's boundaries and about her personal space and how that is important to her.
- Suggest that Jenna be honest with her friend that she is not comfortable with the tickling and to find a new way to greet that is comfortable for both of them.
- Ask Jenna if she wants you to go with her to speak with Jess about it.
- If touch is triggering Jenna on serious issues, ask if you can get her some help.

## 9 The Smother

Preston has an adorable baby brother. Whenever Preston invites you and Shamila over, Shamila likes to pick up Preston's baby brother and smother him with hugs and kisses.

- Do nothing; babies need to be loved.
- Ask Preston if his baby brother likes all that attention.
- Make a point of asking Preston and his mom how to tell if the baby is happy or uncomfortable.
- Explain to Shamila that even babies know how they feel about touch and have boundaries from a young age.
- Suggest to Shamila that she might have to find another way to interact with the baby.
- Suggest to Shamila that she talk to Preston and his mom about the best way to treat the baby.

## 10 No Nudes

Kim and Ming break up. Kim shares with you that she found out that Ming is sharing with his friends the nude photos that she sent Ming of herself.

- Do nothing; the more people that get involved, the worse it will be.
- Tell Kim that what Ming is doing is against the law, since she never gave him permission to show the pictures to others.
- Offer to go with Kim to talk to Ming.
- Suggest that Kim report Ming to the social media site.
- Tell a trusted adult and have them explain to Ming that he is breaking the law.

- The age of online digital consent is thirteen years old.

- If you share a private video or photo of someone underage, you can be charged with distribution of child pornography.

# More Help

It takes time, critical thinking, and sensitivity to learn the skills in this book. There are many ways to manage consent and to deal with conflicts about it, but in the end, what is most important is that everyone feels safe and comfortable.

If you need more information or someone to talk to, these resources might help.

### Help Organizations
Kids Help Phone  1-800-668-6868

Child and Adolescent Services for Abuse and Trauma (CASAT)  416-603-1827

Toronto Rape Crisis Centre  416-597-8808

Children's Aid Society of Toronto  416-924-4646

Catholic Children's Aid Society of Toronto  416-395-1500

Native Child and Family Services  416-969-8510

Jewish Child and Family Services  416-638-7800

Toronto Police Services  416-808-2222

### Websites
Kids Help Phone  www.kidshelpphone.ca

Community Legal Clinics  www.legalaid.on.ca

Justice for Children and Youth  www.jfcy.org

Boost Child & Youth Advocacy Centre  www.boostforkids.org

Project Consent: https://www.projectconsent.com/

Teen Talk: https://teentalk.ca/learn-about/consent-2/

Planned Parenthood Toronto: http://www.ppt.on.ca/

### Kids' Books
*Let's Talk About Body Boundaries, Consent and Respect: Teach children about body ownership* by Jayneen Sanders

*What Does Consent Really Mean?* by Pete Wallis, Joseph Wilkins, and Thalia Wallis

*C is for Consent* by Eleanor Morrison and Faye Orlove

Copyright © 2020 by Keisha Evans and N.B. Gonsalvez
Illustrations © 2020 by James Lorimer & Company

Published in Canada in 2020.
Published in the United States in 2020.

James Lorimer & Company Ltd., Publishers acknowledges funding support from the Ontario Arts Council (OAC), an agency of the Government of Ontario. We acknowledge the support of the Canada Council for the Arts, which last year invested $153 million to bring the arts to Canadians throughout the country. This project has been made possible in part by the Government of Canada and with the support of Ontario Creates.

Series design: Blair Kerrigan/Glyphics
Cover design: Gwen North, Tyler Cleroux
Cover image: Shutterstock

**Library and Archives Canada Cataloguing in Publication**

Title: Consent : deal with it before boundaries get crossed / Keisha Evans and N.B. Gonsalvez
  ; illustrated by Jenny Chan.
Names: Evans, Keisha, author. | Gonsalvez, N. B., author.
Identifiers: Canadiana 20190186895 | ISBN 9781459415065 (hardcover)
Subjects: LCSH: Sexual consent—Juvenile literature. | LCSH: Sexual ethics—Juvenile literature.
Classification: LCC HQ32 .E93 2020 | DDC j176/.4—dc23

James Lorimer & Company Ltd., Publishers
117 Peter Street, Suite 304
Toronto, ON, Canada, M5V 0M3
www.lorimer.ca

Distributed in Canada by:
Formac Lorimer Books
5502 Atlantic Street
Halifax, NS, Canada
B3H 1G4

Distributed in the US by:
Lerner Publisher Services
1251 Washington Ave. N.
Minneapolis, MN, USA
55401
www.lernerbooks.com

Printed and bound in China.